Published by Creative Paperbacks
P.O. Box 227, Mankato, Minnesota 56002
Creative Paperbacks is an imprint of
The Creative Company
www.thecreativecompany.us

Design by The Design Lab
Production by Chelsey Luther
Art direction by Rita Marshall
Printed in the United States of America

Photographs by Alamy (imagebroker), Dreamstime
(Beritk, Blueximages, Michael Elliott, Eric Gevaert,
Shawn Jackson, Katerika), Getty Images (Todd
Lawson), Shutterstock (Eric Isselee, Maxim Petrichuk,
Mariia Savoskula), SuperStock (Ed Darack, Hemis.
fr, Norbert Probst/imageb/imagebroker.net, Steve
Bloom Images)

Library of Congress Cataloging-in-Publication Data
Riggs, Kate.
Camels / Kate Riggs.
p. cm. — (Amazing animals)
Summary: A basic exploration of the appearance,
behavior, and habitat of camels, hump-backed, furry
desert-dwellers. Also included is a story from folklore
explaining how camels got their humps.
Includes bibliographical references and index.
ISBN 978-1-60818-346-3 (hardcover)
ISBN 978-0-89812-925-0 (pbk)
1. Camels—Juvenile literature. I. Title. II. Series:
Amazing animals.

QL737.U54R54 2014
599.63'62—dc23   2013002864

First Edition
9 8 7 6 5 4 3 2 1

AMAZING ANIMALS
CAMELS
BY KATE RIGGS

CREATIVE PAPERBACKS

This dromedary lives in the Sahara Desert of Africa

A camel is a furry **mammal**. There are two kinds of camels. Dromedaries (*DRAH-meh-dare-eez*) live in **deserts** in the Middle East and northern Africa. Bactrian camels live in grasslands or deserts in Asia.

deserts hot, dry places that do not get much rain

mammal an animal that has hair or fur and feeds its babies with milk

Dromedaries have

one hump on their back. Bactrian camels have two humps. A camel's hump stores fat. It does not have any bones.

Camels have two toes on each foot with loose skin in between

Camels are six to seven feet (1.8–2.1 m) tall. They weigh more than 1,000 pounds (453 kg). Male camels are usually bigger than female camels.

A camel's hump adds up to 12 inches (30.5 cm) to its height

Camel fur can be made into clothing and rugs

Many camels live in hot places.

Their fur helps keep them from getting sunburned. Bactrian camels have longer fur than dromedaries. Camels have thick eyelashes. The eyelashes protect their eyes from snow in the **mountains** and dust in the desert.

mountains very big hills made of rock

Camels eat plants. They eat tall grasses, woody twigs, and prickly desert plants. Camels use the front teeth in their lower jaw to grab plants. Then they chew with their back teeth.

Camels have special tongues that help them eat prickly plants

A newborn camel
is about 3.5 feet
(1 m) tall

A mother camel has one **calf** at a time. Calves do not have humps when they are born. Their eyes are open and they can stand. Calves drink their mothers' milk until they are a year old.

calf a baby camel

Most wild camels live in small groups called herds. Female camels and calves make up some herds. Male camels live by themselves or with other males. People keep tame camels in pens. Camels can live for 30 to 50 years.

*A herd usually has
2 to 15 camels in it*

Camels eat plants whenever they can find them. A camel can eat about nine pounds (4 kg) of food each day. It can drink about 50 gallons (189 l) of water in a day! When a camel does not get enough food or water, its body uses up the fat in its hump.

*Camels are good at
sharing food and water*

People use camels to carry heavy loads. People ride camels, too. In countries that do not have wild camels, people go to zoos and circuses to see them. It is fun to see these hump-backed animals up-close!

A camel can carry up to 600 pounds (272 kg) of weight

A *Camel Story*

How did camels get their humps? A writer named Rudyard Kipling told a story about this. When the world was new, all the animals had jobs. But the camel was too lazy. He did not want to do any work. He said "Humph!" if anyone asked him to work. He said "Humph!" so many times that the word turned into a lump on his back! The camel has had a hump ever since.

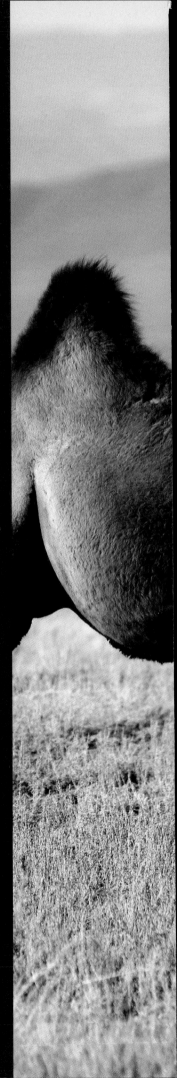

Read More

Borgert-Spaniol, Megan. *Camels*. Minneapolis: Bellwether Media, 2012.

Ganeri, Anita. *I Wonder Why Camels Have Humps and Other Questions about Animals*. Boston: Kingfisher, 2003.

Websites

Camel Coloring Book Pages
http://www.coloring.ws/camel.htm
This page lets you print out pictures of camels to color.

Enchanted Learning: Bactrian Camel
http://www.enchantedlearning.com/subjects/mammals/camel/Bactrian.shtml
This site has facts about the Bactrian camel and a picture to color.